AF372555

Divine Breastfeeding

Our collection

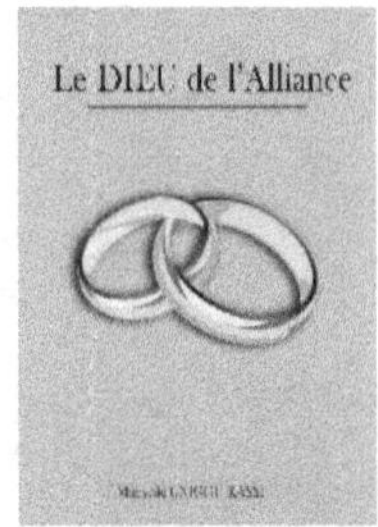

Le DIEU de l'Alliance, February 2016

Le grand saut, October 2016

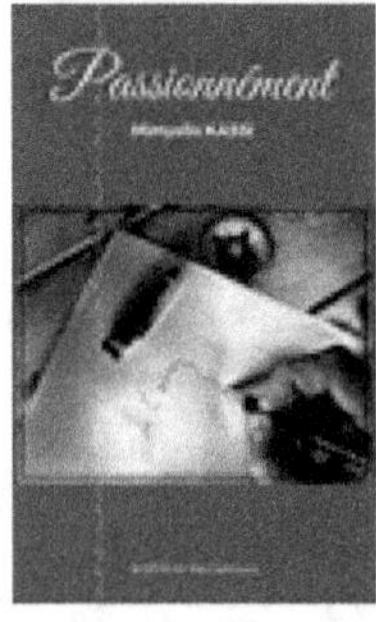

Passionnement, February 2017

La Diligence, March 2017

Témoins Relais, April 2017

21 Jours dans tes parvis, April 2018

Divine Breastfeeding

Translated version of "Allaitement Divin"
Mai 2019

Mimyelle GNIGOU KASSI

Edition : KOEUR de MIEL Editions

ISBN: 979-10-96052-11-0
Mimyelle GNIGOU KASSI
Edition : KOEUR de MIEL Editions
6 rue d'Armaillé, 75017 Paris
Legal Deposit: August 2020
Cover: Kœur de Miel Organisation ©

" For thus saith the Lord, Behold, I will extend peace to her like a river, and the glory of the Gentiles like a flowing stream: then shall ye suck, ye shall be borne upon her sides, and be dandled upon her knees. "

Isaiah 66:12.

I dedicate this book to all those who thirst for GOD.
Let the GOD of the Covenant give us drink of His Divine milk, so that
strengthened by this food we may accomplish what HE expects of
us. He is faithful, He will do it.

*"That you may be nourished and satisfied with the milk of his
consolations, that you may enjoy the fullness of his Glory.*
Isaiah 66:11

Foreword

"As newborn babes, desire the sincere milk of the word, that ye may grow thereby: If so be ye have tasted that the Lord is gracious ".

1 Peter : 2.2-3

It is after the birth of my second son in July 2012, that the Lord inspired me to write this book on divine breastfeeding.

I use the word "breastfeeding" because it's the type of feeding that fits the idea of the book - *therefore, whenever feeding is mentioned, the reader should understand that it strictly refers to breastfeeding.*

From then on, I began my research and set out to publish this book, which I would like to be as accessible as it is profound.

I particularly like the image of breastfeeding, which will take precedence here, because it brings a child into a perfect figure of fragility and innocence. And its mother, a figure of protection and love, all this around the vital notion of food.

It is a perfect reflection of the relationship between GOD and His children,who describes Himself throughout the Holy Scriptures as a loving Father who cares for His sheep.

"Divine Brestfeeding" will therefore make this parallel between these two emblematic images, in order to take us into another dimension of the relationship with GOD.

May the Holy Spirit allow you, dear reader, to grasp the full scope of the message that the Lord wanted to transmit to you in this 5th book of the Collection "Notebooks of the Christian Missionary", and the 7th of our writings.

The collection of "*Christian Missionary Notebooks*" is made up of booklets accessible at all levels (language, thickness, price, spirituality) which make them easy to read. They present several themes useful to Christian daily life, so that the children of GOD can use them as "spiritual reminders", and remain clinging to the vision,

the mission. For when the Lord returns, He will have to find His church ready. *"And I John saw the holy city, the new Jerusalem, coming down out of heaven from God, prepared as a bride adorned for her husband.* **Revelation 21:2**.

<u>Definition of the vision</u>: To keep the crown of life prepared for us, and to enter the Kingdom of Heaven.

"I'm coming soon. Hold fast what you have, so that no one can take your crown of victory from you". **Revelation 3:11**

<u>Objective of the mission</u>: The Great Commission.

"Jesus came to them and said, "All power has been given to me in heaven and on earth. Go [therefore] and make disciples of all nations, baptizing them in the name of the Father and of the Son and of the Holy Spirit, and teaching them to do all that I have commanded you. And I am with you always, even to the end of the world. **"Matthew 28:18-20.**

Enjoy your reading!

Introduction

Breastfeeding is by far the most recommended feeding method by child-related institutions and health specialists. There are several reasons for this. It is available, of very good quality and has unprecedented advantages for the good development of the newborn child.

Just as GOD's Love for Humans is the best formula that can be received by the child of GOD.

Throughout this book, we will make an analysis of breastfeeding that we will put in parallel with the love and the relationship between GOD and Men.

To do so, we will look at the characteristics of breastfeeding, why we need it? then at the rules of Divine breastfeeding, what are the principles to be respected? with a skylight on the post-breastfeeding stage at the end.

As a reminder, as stated above, the reader should note that whenever the word breastfeeding is used, it will refer strictly to breastfeeding (as the word "breastfed" does).

Shall we?

CHAPTER I: Characteristics of Divine Breastfeeding

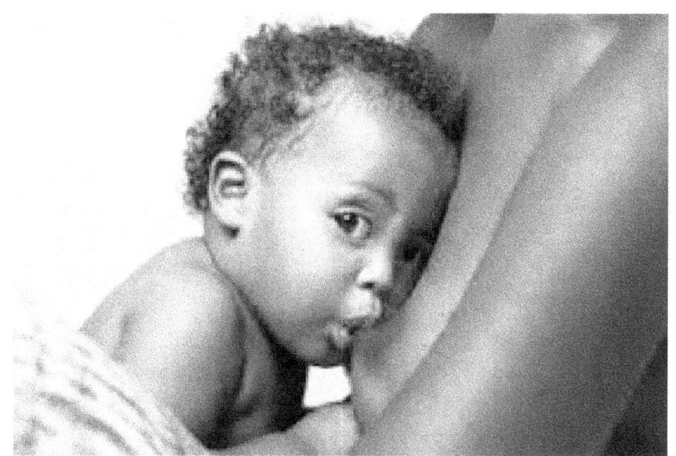

CHAPTER I: Characteristics of Divine Breastfeeding

Breast milk is generally the first food that every human being discovers. If only because it is free and available. It is an indispensable food to feed the infant's small stomach, which needs a complete and balanced food in liquid form for its growth. For this reason, it is good to consider the interest of mother's milk: its richness and characteristics, in order to be able to realize the benefits of Divine Breastfeeding.

This section will help us understand why we need to benefit from Divine Breastfeeding and what its characteristics and benefits are.

"Does a woman forget the child she is breastfeeding? Does she not pity the fruit of her womb? When she forgets it, I will not forget you". Isaiah 49:15.

I.   <u>Free of charge</u>

"Come, buy and eat, come, buy wine and milk, without money, without paying for anything! ». Isaiah: 55:1.

It seems obvious that one of the main advantages of breastfeeding is the free and unlimited availability of breast milk. Indeed, it comes directly from the mother's body. The innate sucking reflex allows the newborn to suck, swallow and feed immediately after birth, making it easier.

According to an analysis published by UNICEF (United Nations International Children's Emergency), the rate of infants being breastfed at least once is much higher in low- and middle-income countries. Thus, the Lord, in creating the woman's body, made sure that no baby dies of hunger or suffers from malnutrition in its early hours. He has provided every woman in childbirth with the ability to breastfeed her child, to bring it at least to an age that allows it to eat solid food.

Just like mother's milk, GOD's grace is available to all those who accept to receive it. It is free and available in unlimited quantities just like GOD's Love.

Throughout the Holy Scriptures, the Lord proposes to His people to come and consume at His source, in a gracious manner and thus benefit from His aura and graces.

JESUS Himself tells us that He is the Bread of Life, He gives Himself freely as food, so that we may have life in abundance. *"For my flesh is food indeed, and my blood is drink indeed"*. **John: 6:55.**

GOD offers us to be our source.

Yet studies show that despite free breastfeeding, one in five infants in rich countries is not breastfed, compared to only one in 25 in low- and middle-income countries.

In the same way, in spite of the availability and gratuity of the Love that comes from God, very often we prefer a pale imitation of the happiness and well-being He wants to offer us, just as infant milk is a pale imitation of mother's milk. Of course, like any imitation, the benefits are sometimes inadequate, limited in duration and above all fail to satisfy our needs in the long run (not to mention what it costs us). What a pity, what a waste!

Make the choice of free and excellent: Choose Divine Breastfeeding!

"Thus you will be filled with the consolations she gives you, like infants who are breastfed by their mother, suckling with delight from her bountiful womb. Isaiah: 66:11

II. <u>The abundant quantity</u>

"« …. I have come that the sheep may have life, and that they may have it in abundance". John 10:10.

The second characteristic that we want to address is the unlimited quantity available, that is, the abundance of breast milk. Indeed, during pregnancy, certain hormones prepare the breasts for breastfeeding. For example, breastfeeding triggers the mother's release of prolactin, a hormone that stimulates milk production and helps ensure a continuous food supply for the newborn.

The previous verse tells us that the Lord in His goodness wants us to enjoy everything we need in abundance. This is even the reason why He came to this earth. Indeed, He, who is an infinite, unlimited and eternal GOD, can only offer His children things of the same nature as Him, that is to say, food in unlimited quantity.

Opting for Divine Breastfeeding means choosing to taste the eternal flavours and delights of our GOD.

« For thus saith the Lord, Behold, I will extend peace to her like a river, and the glory of the Gentiles like a flowing stream: then shall ye suck, ye shall be borne upon her sides, and be dandled upon her knees.
As one whom his mother comforteth, so will I comfort you; and ye shall be comforted in Jerusalem ». Isaiah 66 : 12-13

III.   <u>The ideal quality</u>

"If you then, evil as you are, know how to give good things to your children, how much more will your father in heaven give good things to those who ask him? **Matthew 7:11.**

At birth, breasts secrete colostrum. This first milk, orange-yellow, is very precious for the child. It contains a large amount of vitamins, minerals and antibodies, which protect the baby from infections. Breast milk ingested by newborns during the first few days of life (the famous colostrum) is extremely rich in nutrients and antibodies and acts as the child's first vaccine, providing a vital shield of protection against disease.

Breast milk has an ideal composition, it contains three times less proteins than cow's milk and contains proteins such as methionine, taurine or tyrosine, which respond to the child's enzymatic immaturity. It also contains three times less calcium. It contains three times more lactose than cow's milk. A litre of breast milk provides two to nine times more unsaturated fatty acids than a litre of semi-skimmed industrial cow's milk. These unsaturated fatty acids are essential for brain development and the human body does not know how to make them. Cow's milk provides half as much iron as mother's milk, which is already at the lower limit of requirements. Compared to cow's milk, vitamin levels are higher in breast milk, except for folic acid (identical) and vitamin K (lower in breast milk). Vitamin C levels are only adequate if the mother does not smoke. Women's milk is also very rich in vitamin E, a powerful antioxidant.

It's amazing how rich breast milk is. This richness is no longer in doubt, it is a fact that has been proven worldwide.

The Lord who created us knows exactly what we need. He makes sure that the infant receives from his mother the necessary and essential nutrients for life.

Likewise, throughout our life, the best source of blessings, necessary for a fulfilled life, can only be GOD.

Very often GOD's demands are wrongly considered as burdens and brakes on our "freedom". But in reality, everything the Lord asks us not to do is only to ensure a peaceful life. Otherwise, if we want to be pragmatic: how does flying undermine GOD's sovereignty in heaven? It is you who steal that will end up going to prison and tarnish part of your history!

In what way does the fact that you are an adulterer harm the integrity of GOD in heaven? (Especially since your image does not reflect His image, since you are not His only child). It is rather to avoid you the humiliation of a scandal or the moral wound of sin.

In short, to say that the Lord only wants our happiness, he never ceases to repeat it to us, and his ordinances have the sole purpose of ensuring our well-being on the earth he has given us and during this life he has given us. And even when faced with the most complex situations in our lives, He does not abandon us. His faithfulness always comes through in the end.

 "They *that turn away from me shall be written in the earth, for they have forsaken the fountain of living water, the Lord*". Jeremiah 17:13

Then let us desire with all our heart, the Divine milk, He said that it is the source of living water and he who drinks from its source will never thirst again.

At this point, I would like to stop and let you take a few minutes of prayer, where you will make a heart to heart with GOD, and where with your own words, you will express to Him your thirst for His divine milk, and your desire to be watered at His source. If you want, you can mark your personal prayer here:

....

....

....

....

"Desire, like newborn children, the spiritual and pure milk, that through it you may grow for salvation. 1 Peter: 2.2

IV.   <u>An evolutionary and adequate composition</u>

"God can fill you with all His graces so that you may <u>always</u> have in <u>every respect enough to satisfy all your needs</u> and still have plenty for every good work. **2 Corinthians 9:8.**

Breast milk is exactly tailored to the baby's needs so that there is no metabolic   waste.
It is adapted to the baby's physiology as seen above.

The composition of breast milk changes during breastfeeding to suit the infant's needs and also varies according to the mother's diet. The taste of the milk may also change, allowing the baby to get used to different flavours. Breast milk contains more than 200 components.

According to an American study, mother's milk is even adapted according to the baby's sex: richer in fat and protein for baby boys, in greater quantities for baby girls.

It's so surprising! Because when we say that the composition of breast milk adapts to the needs of the baby, that is to say that if one day the baby, for whatever reason, has a need for magnesium, for example to improve his health, automatically, breast milk, in the mother's body (when it is no longer in contact with the baby's body), produces exactly the amount of magnesium that baby needs. If on another day, the baby lacks Iron, depending for example on his age development, the mother's body automatically produces the new amount of Iron required by baby.

One is almost tempted to ask how the mother's body knows that the child's needs have evolved in this or that direction? and how can it adapt so precisely?

"...For your Father knows what you need, before you even ask him."
Matthew 6.8

JEHOVAH is the one who created us according to His divine plan and He knows exactly what we need and He has the means to fill us with exactly what we really need, at the very moment when the need arises. Will we have enough faith and confidence to turn to Him and wait for Him the Divine milk?

"For I know the plans that I have made for you, says the Lord, plans for peace and not for evil, to give you a future and a hope. Jeremiah 29:11

CHAPTER II: Divine Breastfeeding Rules

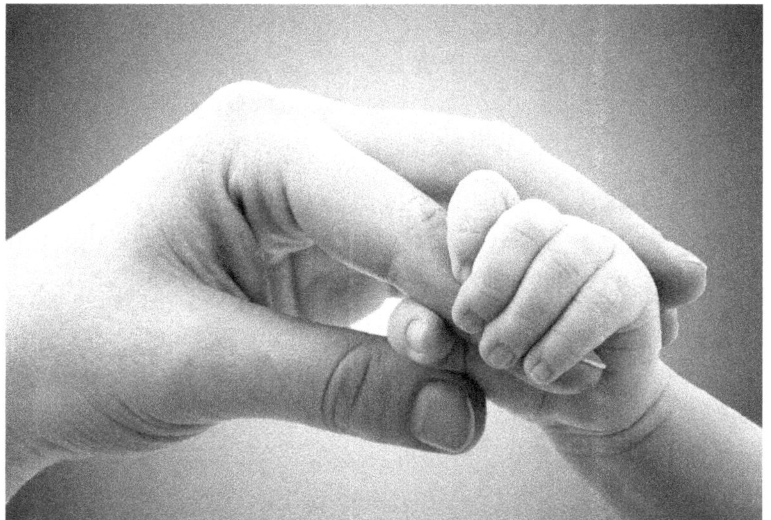

<u>CHAPTER II</u>: Divine Breastfeeding Rules

*"**Bring me back to life according to your goodness, that I may keep the commandments of your mouth**". Psalm 119:88.*

The Bible describes our GOD as a GOD of order and discipline. He takes care to give us what we need, in sufficient quantity and quality, in order to ensure our evolution and growth. However, in order to have access to this fullness, there are attitudes that we must adopt.

As with the characteristics, there are also rules that govern Divine Breastfeeding. We have listed 4 of them that we will go through together in detail:

- The contact

- The look

- Rest

- Dependency

I.   <u>The contact of prayer</u>

"Pray without ceasing." 1 Thessalonians: 5.17

One of the obvious characteristics of breastfeeding, especially maternal breastfeeding, is contact. At the time of feeding, there is necessarily contact: either from the baby's mouth with the mother's nipple, or from the baby's body resting on the mother's body (via the arm, via the open foot ...).

Apart from this oral contact, there is what is called "skin-to-skin". This involves placing the baby, bare skin against its mother, who is also bare skin.
The vast majority of newborns can be put on skin-to-skin and have access to the breast within minutes of birth. In fact, scientists show that many babies as young as a few minutes old, when put skin to skin, are able to crawl to the breast, take it, and begin to suck on their own.

Research shows that skin-to-skin contact is good and very important for both baby and parent (even when the baby is not breastfeeding). Skin-to-skin contact helps babies adapt to their new environment, their breathing and heart rate are more normal, their blood oxygen saturation is higher, their temperature is more stable and their blood sugar levels are higher. Immediate skin-to-skin contact helps regulate the newborn's body temperature and allows the body to be populated with beneficial bacteria from the mother's skin. These good bacteria provide protection against infection and help strengthen the baby's immune system.

In addition, there is ample evidence that the more babies are kept skin-to-skin in the first days and weeks of life (not just during feedings), the better their brain development will be. It is now thought that a baby's brain develops in a certain way because of this skin-to-skin contact, and this significant growth occurs mainly in the first 3-8 weeks of life.

In fact, early childhood specialists say that these little rubs, these touches, these contacts create a special relationship between mother and child, which will also determine their future relationships and the emotional development of the child.

It is the same with Divine Breastfeeding. Contact is essential for a good relationship with GOD. Contact is what will facilitate the reception of Divine milk, and above all, will increase your intimacy with GOD and your emotional development. And contact is established by a constant and diligent life of prayer. *"Pray without ceasing"*.

The most important thing is not so much the words we align, but the presence to GOD, that is, the love with which we present ourselves before GOD, and take pleasure in His presence. Of course, not everyone starts by praying for several hours in a row, but it is the constancy and perseverance that you will show to respect those 10 minutes of daily prayers that will qualify you for greater moments of prayer. Indeed, GOD will come to the rescue of your weakness and will reward your efforts of Fidelity. Without you realizing it, you will begin to desire to stay longer in the presence of GOD. Ten minutes will seem insufficient to you. It is the manifestation of GOD's Faithfulness towards us.

The Lord promised never to abandon us. It's up to us to accept his proposal and let him into our lives.

"« …. And behold, I am with you always, until the end of time. " **Matthew 28:20.**

You can now formulate a prayer, and ask GOD for the grace to never break this contact, the bond of prayer, but rather to be a man or woman of prayer.

....

....

....

....

II.   <u>The look of complicity and hope</u>

"The eyes of all wait for you, and you give them food in its time." **Psalms: 145.15**

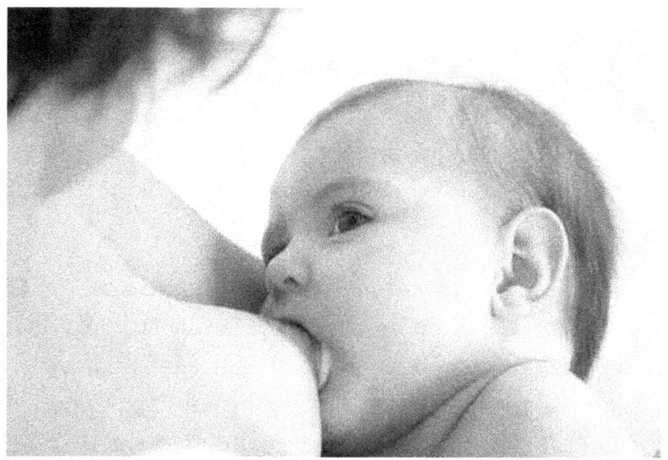

During feeding, baby tends to look into his mother's eyes. Midwives and other child specialists say that it is a privileged moment of exchange with the mother, which contributes to the bond between mother and child.

The gaze is characteristic of trust, hope and also love.

Remember that GOD's gaze is merciful, compassionate and full of love. Peter meets the gaze of JESUS Christ after betraying him. This creates in him the desire for repentance.

It is important to plunge your gaze into the pool of love, in the gaze of Christ.

Raising our eyes to GOD translates our hope in Him. In every situation we go through, in great joys as well as in great trials, we must keep our eyes fixed on GOD. Indeed, many people mistakenly think that it is only when we are troubled that we must look to GOD. This is not true. Even when we are in joy because we have been the subject of a very great blessing, when we are being drunk with Divine milk, it is precisely at that moment that we must keep our eyes fixed on GOD. It is then a gaze of thanksgiving, gratitude and love that we give Him, and our relationship with Him is even more intensified.

Of course, when we are also in moments of extreme doubt, or in difficulties as the Psalmist says : "in the valley of shadow and death", it is GOD's gaze that meets our gaze, that makes us "fear no evil". In these circumstances, it is rather a look of hope and of asking for help that we address to Him, proving to Him that we have Faith in His love for us. Of course, He who is Good and Faithful cannot abandon us to our fate.

Finally, to plunge his gaze into that of our source, the Lord JESUS, allows us to improve our relations with our brothers. Indeed, there may come times when we are hurt, outraged and even persecuted by our brothers in Christ or outside the church, our human brothers simply. And the natural reflex of man in general is to react to this offence. But Christ comes to tell us in the Gospel, "if you are hit on the left cheek, stretch out your right cheek as well". This seems paradoxical and unjust. However, when we look with the eyes of Christ, we realize that the one who oppresses us is in reality himself, a victim of lack of love or lack of trust in him, the condemnation disappears to make way for compassion. Because for GOD, each person is a soul, for whom He shed His blood on the cross, that he might be saved. Even as a sinner, GOD would like to see her saved, before the day of judgment comes and it is too late. "I hate sin, but I love the sinner". Otherwise, the sacrifice of the cross would have been in vain for her. That is why GOD missions Christians to go out into the world to proclaim the Good News.

The gaze is also the characteristic of the complicity we have with our Source, our Father.

We must keep our eyes on our GOD when we want to enjoy the fullness of Divine Breastfeeding.

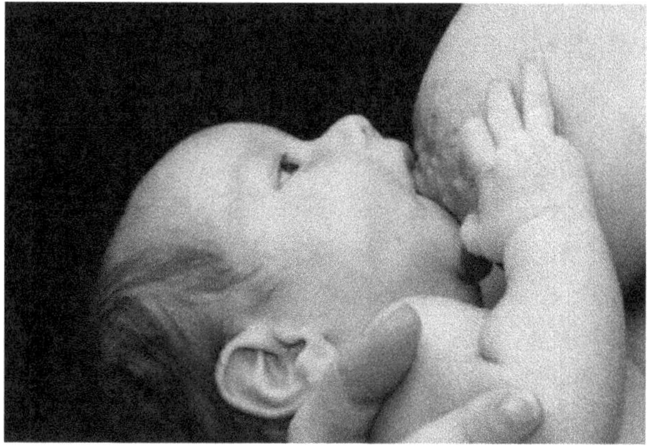

"I lift up my eyes to thee, Who sitteth in heaven."

Psalms: 123.1

III. The repose of trust

"You shall suck the milk of the nations, you shall suck the teats of kings; and you shall know that I am the LORD your saviour, your redeemer, the mighty one of Jacob. Isaiah 60:16

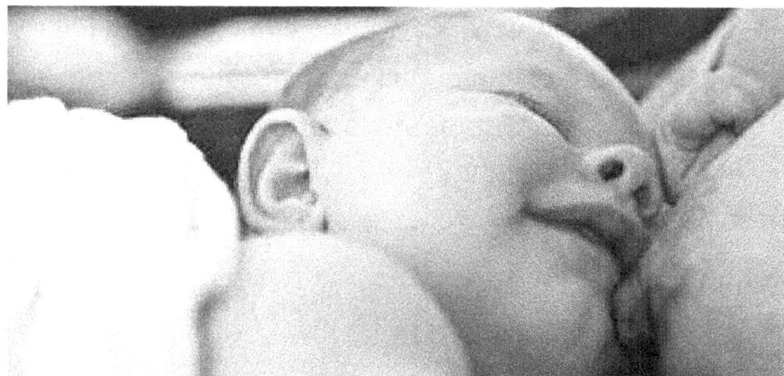

Feeding does not only meet a baby's need for food: it also serves to reassure him. During breastfeeding, the mother and baby form a lasting bond. During feeding, all of the baby's senses are awakened. Many elements remind him of his intrauterine life. He/She is at peace.

When we want to live from Divine Breastfeeding, we must learn to rest in Christ, who died so that we may have life. The Bible says that JESUS carried our burdens on the cross-post, and it is by his bruises that we are healed. The Christian who is fed at GOD's breast, must learn to rest with GOD.

For the one who opts for divine breastfeeding, it is important to have Trust in GOD. It is because mothers know that breast milk is better for their children that they make this choice. The Christian who decides to give his life to GOD must be conscious, and I repeat CONSCIOUS, that the best thing that can happen to him is the will of GOD in his life, and even when this will passes through moments of difficulty, shadows resembling valleys of death, we must continue to believe that the Staff and the Hood of GOD are there and this must reassure us (Ps 91). The Christian often panics even more than the one who has no hope, even though Christ is our hope, He promised that He would be with us to the end.

Whatever storms and shipwrecks you are going through right now, learn to rely on GOD. The Bible says in Psalm 23, *even when I pass through the valley of the shadow of death, I shall not do any evil, for thy rod and thy staff reassure me.*

No situation is new under the sun. In the 6,000 years that the earth has existed and that He is GOD, rest assured that the Lord has already been confronted with a situation similar to what you are experiencing and may be even worse. You cannot surprise Him with a case and none of your problems can make Him panic.

Then why are you panicking? Since when does a baby who's being breastfed panic when his mother's calm?

Enter into the rest of GOD!
Rest in the arms of your GOD!

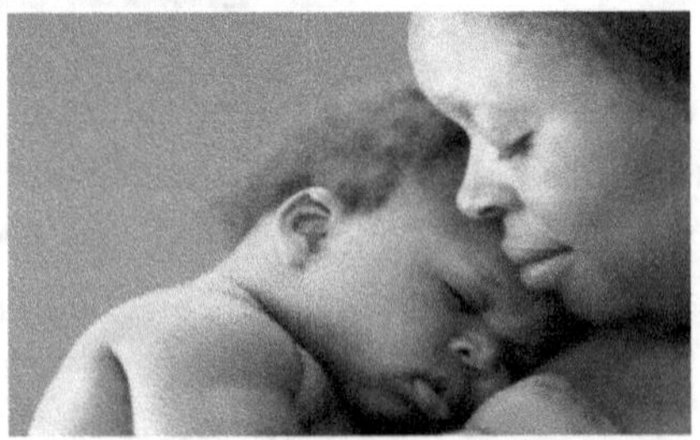

"So don't worry, saying, 'What are we going to eat? What are we going to drink? What are we going to wear to dress?". It's the heathens who are always looking for all that. But your Father in heaven knows that you need it. <u>Concern yourself first with the Kingdom of God and the righteous life that it asks for, and God will grant you everything else as well</u>. So don't worry about tomorrow: tomorrow will worry about itself. To each day is enough sorrow". **Matthew 6:31-34.**

IV.   <u>Dependency</u>

"As the branch cannot bear fruit by itself unless it remains attached to the vine, neither can you bear fruit unless you remain in me.
I am the vine, you are the branches. He who abides in me and in whom I abide bears much fruit, for <u>without me you can do nothing</u>".
John: 15:4-5.

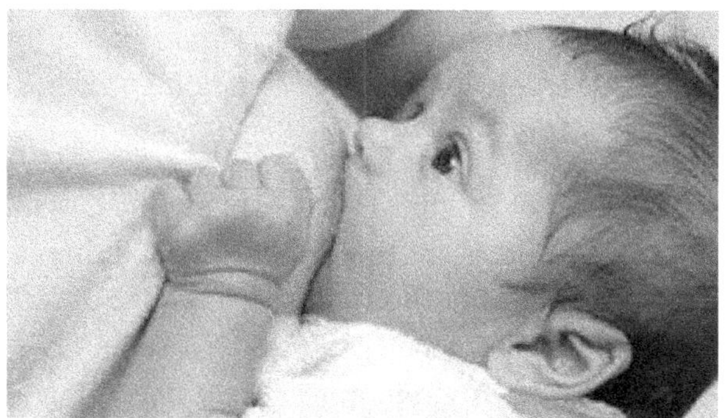

When parents opt for exclusive breastfeeding, a relationship of dependence of the child on the mother follows. This is because the baby is entirely dependent on the mother and no one else. The mother will be the one to determine her baby's future growth through her own nutrition and lifestyle. The baby does not have the means to count on a Plan B that he will have put aside in case the mother's will is not in line with her own baby's will. On the contrary, the milk production and content is ideal for the baby.

The World Health Organization (WHO) and UNICEF recommend that breastfeeding should begin within one hour of birth and that infants should be exclusively breastfed for the first six months of life. This means that the infant does not take in any other food or liquid, not even water, as long as breastmilk is sufficiently rich and already meets all the baby's nutritional needs, protects infants from infectious and respiratory diseases and strengthens their immune system.

The same applies to Divine Breastfeeding. The Christian who wants to drink at the source of GOD and be protected and strengthened by the precious Divine beverage must depend exclusively on Him. He must have no other support than GOD.

In the verse stated above, Christ is defined as the central element for our life. **Without HIM we can do nothing. He invites us to choose HIM as the PRIORITY of our life.**

"He who loves his father or mother more than I am is not worthy of me; he who loves his son or daughter more than I am is not worthy of me. **Matthew 10:37**

Christ wants to be the center of everything. One can find this hard and even a little "selfish" on the part of GOD. But in reality, it is for the good of mankind that the Lord is asking this. Detachment from the things of the world is necessary so that satan does not have a support to attack us. The tempter is like a devouring lion roaming around, waiting to find a loophole. *"Be sober, watch. Your opponent, the devil, prowls around like a roaring lion, looking for whom he will devour.* **1 Peter: 5.8.**

It is important that through spiritual exercises, asceticism, youth and other forms of spiritual discipline, the Christian should detach himself as much as possible from the things of this world, so that satan, as with JESUS, may find nothing of him in us: *"And he cried with a loud voice, saying, What is there between me and you, Jesus, Son of the Most High God? ..."* **Mark: 5:7**.

It reminds me of the examples we often see in action movies where the brave man goes to great lengths not to show his attachment to the people he cares about, for fear that his detractors will get the better of him. Beware, it is not a question of being insensitive or indifferent. It is about putting GOD first in his life.

Addiction can be frightening, even panicky, but in spiritual matters, it is a sine equa none criterion for growth - we talk about it in more detail in the book "The Great Leap".

You cannot acquire the basic rudiments, necessary for your spiritual as well as material evolution, if you do not reach the stage of dependence on GOD. He is the source and origin of all achievement and success.

So, if you have tried everything by your strength, by your knowledge, by your relationships, and you have not reached the satisfaction of your heart, then try with GOD. Try TOTAL ABANDONMENT to GOD. Trust Him completely to solve the knot of your story, and you will see that you have a GOD in heaven who can do infinitely more than we can hope or imagine. (**Ephesians 3:20**).

"I won't leave you orphans, I'll come to you".

John 4:10.

Conclusion

At the end of my talk, I would like to remind you that Divine Breastfeeding is indispensable and perfect for the growth of every Man, and this from all points of view (spiritual as well as material).

It is therefore up to us to CHOOSE this way of breastfeeding where our source is the Creator Himself, in order to reach this life of feats to which we are all called.

"For you, who for a long time should have been masters, you still need to be taught the first rudiments of the oracles of God; you have come to need milk and not solid food. **Hebrews 5:12**

Once we are connected to this source and drink Divine milk, we should not forget that we ourselves are called to become a source for our brothers. Didn't the Lord say, *"Out of you I will cause springs of living water to spring forth*? "».

So let us not forget that we are blessed to become, in our turn, blessings for our brothers, and let us work to become so effectively.

May the GOD of the Covenant give us the grace to be able to fulfill with zeal and love this mission of being salt and light for this world. In the Name of JESUS! Amen!

About the author

Mimyelle is married and has wonderful children.

From a very young age, she has had a very special relationship with the Lord and once she arrived at high school, she taught catechism to the youngest, and integrated the charismatic renewal and the choir.

In 2000, as a student at the National Polytechnic Institute - INPHB - of Yamoussoukro, in Ivory Coast, she took part with the Founder ACKAH Bilé Daniel, in his capacity as Head of the [1st] promotion of the Ministry, in the creation of the MICI (*Ministry of Intercession for Ivory Coast which to date has more than 500 members on several continents*). She retains this position and since 2012 until today, she is a member of the council of elders of the MICI.

In 2008, as she was finishing her formation in France, she received a vision from the Lord for women and children and created the mission "School for Life".

She then founded KOEUR de Miel Organisation, an events company specialising in charity and social work through its KOEUR en Or Foundation.

In 2010, she participates with Moderator Epherlin KOFFI, in the creation of CENACLE Organisation, which will become the Missionary Apostolate of CENACLE, as Deputy Leader. The Missionary Apostolate of CENACLE is based on several parishes in Abidjan and in the West African Sub-region.

In the same year, she began courses in Theology for the Laity at the Catholic University of West Africa and graduated three years later.

During all these years at MICI and CENACLE, she took part in evangelization missions and spiritual retreats, as a preacher, but also as an organizer or singer.

Returning to France in 2013, she created the French section of the MICI, with the mission of interceding for the Ivory Coast and also for France. In addition, she takes part in evangelization missions for the Missionary Apostolate of CENACLE.

In 2016, she founded the International Apostolate Generation Deborah - AIGD, present in Europe and Africa.

By training, Mimyelle is an Actuary (graduate in Ivory Coast), and a Risk Management Expert (graduate in France).

Since 2016, she has been writing Christian books for the spiritual edification of the children of GOD.

Some Actions of the Deborah and Lappidoth Generation International Apostolate - AIGDL

<u>Our vision</u>

The International Apostolate Generation Deborah and Lappidoth has a vision of GIVING (AGAIN) LIFE to this world in crisis, by **awakening a generation with a specific call to leadership, like Deborah and Lappidoth in the Bible (Judges 4)**   .

1st International Gathering of the Amazons of Christ: Generation Deborah (March 2016)

Dedication of the book The GOD of the Covenant

Dinner of Hope - Benefit for underprivileged children

(April 2016)

Evangelism and donations in the village of Kpangouoin -
Western Côte d'Ivoire (August 2016)

Announcing the Gospel - Gifts of food, books and Bibles

1st Testimonial Dinner organized in Europe - Paris (December 2016)

Book Dedication

The GOD of the Alliance &

The Big Jump

Christmas Tree - Man - Ivory Coast (December 2016)

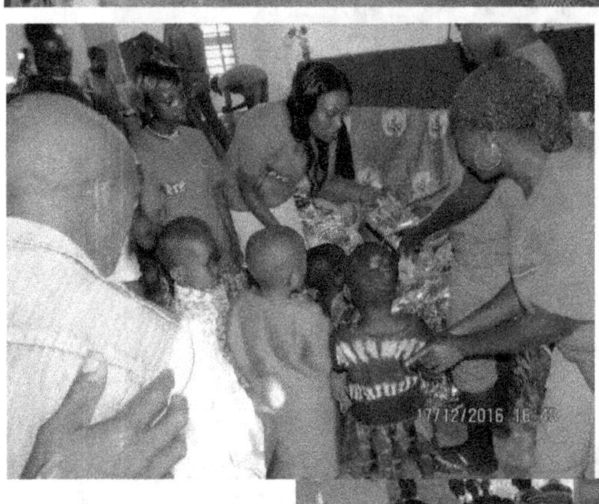

Medical check-ups - Côte d'Ivoire (January 2017)

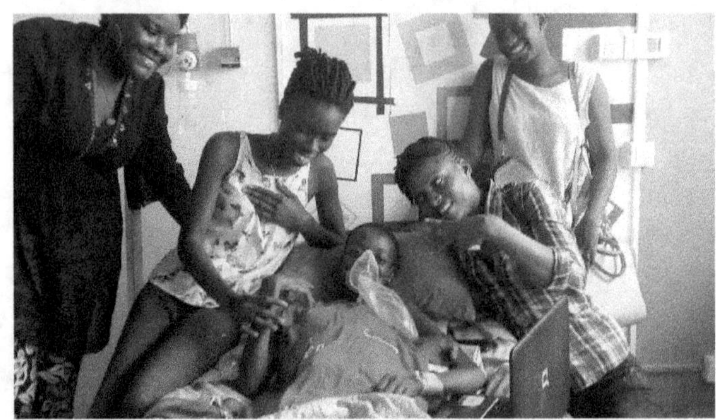

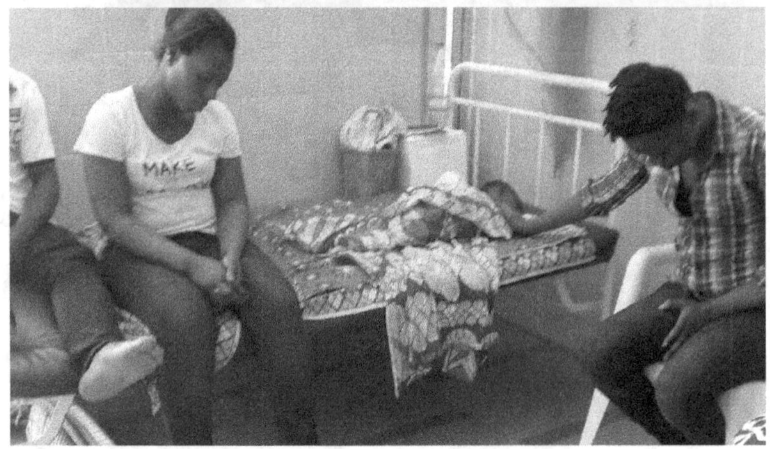

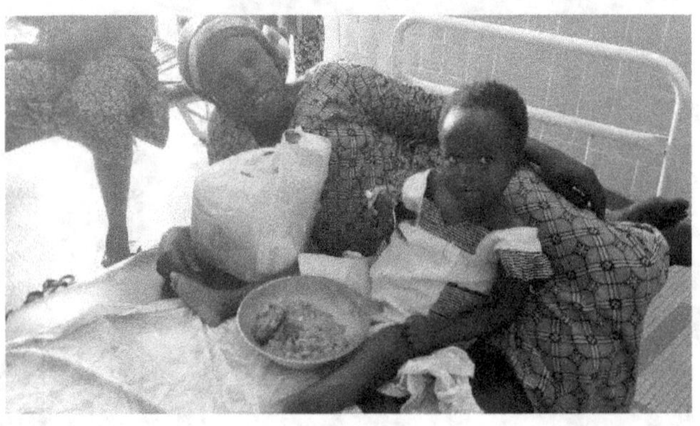

2nd edition of the International Gathering of the Amazons of Christ: Deborah Generation
(April 2017)

Dinner of Hope - Benefit for underprivileged children
(April 2017)

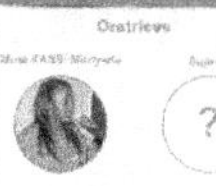

Some Actions of the KOEUR en Or Foundation

"A drop of water to transform lives."

Christmas tree at the NGO la Pépinière de Man - December 2012.

Donations for Christmas to the school " *Ste Thérèse Artisanale de Duekoué* ".
(December 2012)

Concert and donations to Bingerville Psychiatric Hospital
(January 2013)

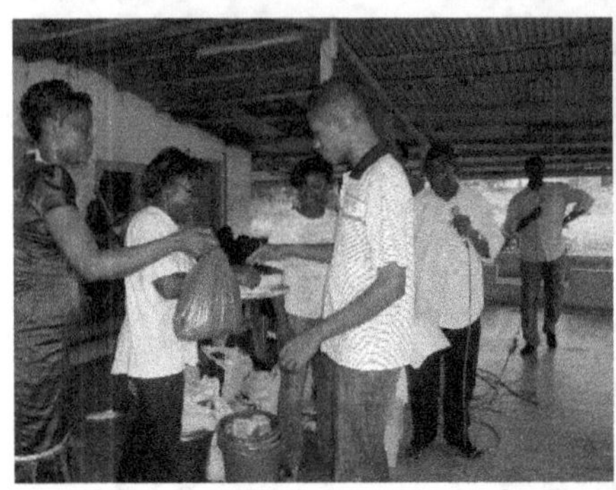

Christmas Tree Partnership
With the GNIGOU Family
at Divo (December 2014)

Easter meal organized at the NGO La Pépinière and delivery of chocolate, food, books and clothes (March 2016)

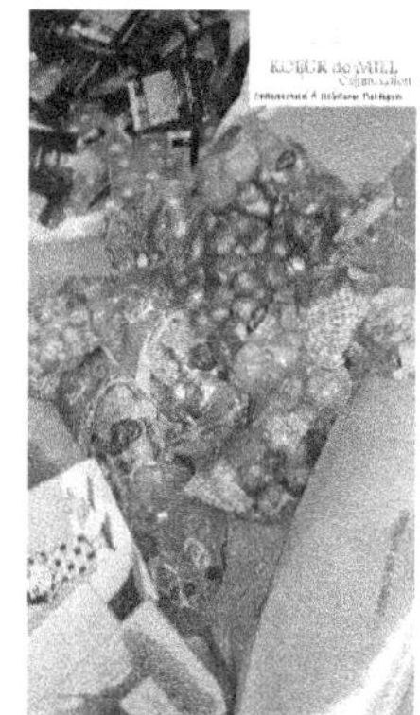

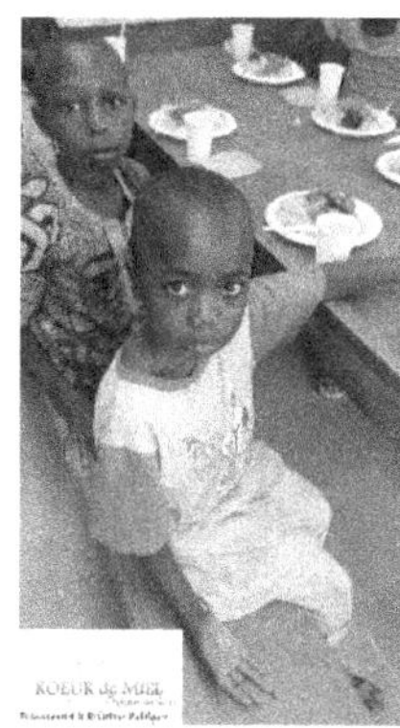

Lunch at Bingerville Psychiatric Hospital (April 2016)

Lunch offered with Youth at Risk (December 2019)

To contact us

KOEUR de MIEL Editions
An entity of the Lyketh & Co Group
6 rue d'Armaillé 75017 Paris
www.lyketh.fr

editions@lyketh.fr

Our works are available worldwide, via the Internet.

You can also contact the following numbers:

France: + 337 82 32 68 29

USA: + 1 (571) 575-5428

Canada: +1 (437) 990-2191

Ivory Coast: + 225 44 28 02 28

+ 225 07 49 12 73

<u>**Koeur en Or Foundation**</u> :

You can contact us if you want to participate in the actions of the Koeur en Or Foundation, you can contact **International Apostolate of the Deborah and Lappidoth Generation** :

France: + 337 82 32 68 29

USA: + 1 (571) 575-5428

Canada: +1 (437) 990-2191

Ivory Coast: + 225 44 28 02 28

+ 225 07 49 12 73

<u>**Facebook**</u>:

Apostolat International Génération Déborah **- AIGLD.**

Don't forget to like and share our publications

Table of Contents

Printed in France